Don't Give Up, Charlie Brown

Selected Cartoons from
YOU'VE HAD IT, CHARLIE BROWN
VOL II

Charles M. Schulz

CORONET BOOKS
Hodder Fawcett, London

First published by Fawcett Publications
Inc., New York, 1974

Coronet edition 1975
Second impression 1976

Printed and bound in Great Britain for
Coronet Books, Hodder Fawcett, London,
by Hazell Watson & Viney Ltd,
Aylesbury, Bucks

ISBN 0 340 19858 3

C'MON, GET A HIT! WE NEED A HIT! OOOO, HOW WE NEED A HIT! PLEASE, GET A HIT...PLEASE...PLEASE...

STRIKE ONE!

STRIKE TWO!

STRIKE THREE!

YOU DIDN'T EVEN SWING! THAT'S GONNA COST YOU HALF YOUR SUPPER TONIGHT!

SNIF!

RATS! WHY CAN'T I BE ROUGH, AND TOUGH AND MEAN LIKE ALL THE OTHER MANAGERS?

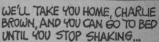

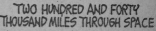

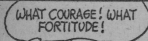

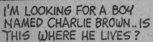

→

IN REGARD TO "BE KIND TO ANIMALS WEEK," I HAVE A QUESTION..

YOU ANIMALS EXPECT TO BE TREATED A LITTLE BIT NICER BY PEOPLE THIS WEEK... RIGHT?

WELL, DOES THIS MEAN THAT YOU, IN TURN, ARE ALSO GOING TO MAKE AN EXTRA EFFORT TO BE MORE KIND TO THAT CAT WHO LIVES NEXT DOOR?

I HATE QUESTIONS LIKE THAT..

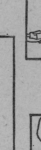

YES, MA'AM, I KNOW THERE ARE SEATS IN THE FRONT ROW... I WAS MERELY OBEYING THE BIBLICAL ADMONITION...

IN THE FOURTEENTH CHAPTER OF LUKE, BEGINNING WITH THE TENTH VERSE, WE READ, "WHEN YOU ARE INVITED, GO AND SIT IN THE LOWEST PLACE SO THAT WHEN YOUR HOST COMES HE MAY SAY TO YOU, 'FRIEND, GO UP HIGHER';"

"...EVERY ONE WHO EXALTS HIMSELF WILL BE HUMBLED, AND HE WHO HUMBLES HIMSELF WILL BE EXALTED."

YES, MA'AM...

MISS OTHMAR ISN'T MUCH FOR BIBLICAL ADMONITIONS...

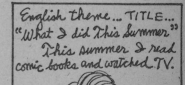

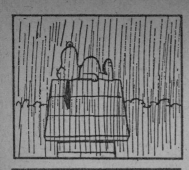

THIS IS THE SORT OF DREARY FALL RAIN THAT MAKES YOU WANT TO SIT INSIDE ALL DAY, AND STARE OUT THE WINDOW, AND DRINK TEA AND PLAY SAD SONGS ON THE STEREO

SO WHY AM I LYING HERE?

ANYONE WHO WOULD SIT AROUND BY HIMSELF MAKING FUNNY FACES MUST BE CRAZY

WHAT ELSE IS THERE TO DO ON A SATURDAY AFTERNOON WHEN YOUR GIRL FRIEND HAS LEFT YOU, YOUR TV SET IS BROKEN AND YOUR JOGGING SUIT IS IN THE WASH?

TOMORROW IS HALLOWEEN, SNOOPY..

TOMORROW NIGHT I'LL BE SITTING HERE IN THIS SINCERE PUMPKIN PATCH, AND I'LL SEE THE 'GREAT PUMPKIN'! HE'LL COME FLYING THROUGH THE AIR, AND I'LL BE HERE TO SEE HIM!

ISN'T THAT EXCITING?

WHEE!

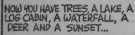

TOMORROW IS BEETHOVEN'S BIRTHDAY..

I HAVE AN IDEA FOR A GREAT PARTY!

WE'LL INVITE AN EQUAL NUMBER OF BOYS AND GIRLS, SEE, AND EACH BOY WILL BRING A GIRL A NICE PRESENT...

→

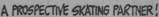

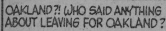

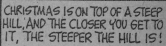

HERE'S THE WORLD WAR I FLYING ACE BACK AT THE AERODROME IN FRANCE..

HE IS SITTING IN THE OFFICERS' CLUB DRINKING ROOT BEER ... IT IS CHRISTMAS DAY, BUT HE IS VERY BITTER...

WILL THIS STUPID WAR NEVER END? MUST I GO ON FLYING THESE MISSIONS FOREVER? I'M TIRED OF THIS WAR!

BESIDES, SANTY DIDN'T BRING ME ANYTHING..

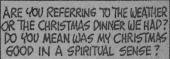

▶→

ALL THIS AND SNOOPY, TOO

All these books are available at your local bookshop or newsagent, or can be ordered direct from the publisher. Just tick the titles you want and fill in the form below.

Prices and availability subject to change without notice.

....

CORONET BOOKS, P.O. Box 11, Falmouth, Cornwall.

Please send cheque or postal order, and allow the following for postage and packing:

U.K. – One book 19p plus 9p per copy for each additional book ordered, up to a maximum of 73p.

B.F.P.O. and EIRE – 19p for the first book plus 9p per copy for the next 6 books, thereafter 3p per book.

OTHER OVERSEAS CUSTOMERS – 20p for the first book and 10p per copy for each additional book.

Name...

Address...

....